Free Verse Editions
Edited by Jon Thompson

For Craig Watson

Contents

4.

5.

Introduction

Perhaps both poetry and history are displacements, appropriations. Of what?

The unnameable ebbs and flows within us, sublime, sometimes malign.

Perhaps displacement and appropriation are forms of confession.

The poet is traveling and she picks up some pulp nonfiction at the airport. The book, badly written, purports to have solved a long mystery, a series of murders. The author dismisses all resolutions but her own, clearly frustrated that other theories continue to exist alongside hers.

Poetry's appropriations are more wily than this, make pun and homonym with other appropriations, disclose and hide personal grief and violation.

How do we create, perpetrate, absorb violence?

The poet, writing, tries on the persona of the perpetrator. She imagines the way that has always been marked as appropriate for her: its demarcations of kind and cruel, assailant and victim, male and female. She scuffs hard at the boundaries, smudging, then defacing them.

She is scared of the poems she writes, hides them.

But some appropriations threaten to become subjugations. She stops fearing the ugliness and fights its power over her. She looks for language, as arch and lyric as it can or wants to be, that remodels presence, gender, the incursion of one being into another. Transformation is, by its very nature, an unsafe process.

The poet finds the book that engendered her inquiry on the floor of a closet, throws it away. The book insists that it has solved the mystery, as though insistence itself were a solution. History looks askance from fact. Appropriation and persona try on possibility as certainty. Transformation is no solution at all.

Rumor

Flesh

When, in the beginning, the word
became flesh, we

wandered for flesh,
believed for it.

> One beginning sits on top
> of another, pinning it down.

We forsook manna for flesh,
winged flesh. We have hunger.

> We hold down our origins,
> tear off their wings,

roast meat until
we become ill of it.

But resignation is not in meat.
We begin ill, but become
more ill.

We cough up words made of flesh
and eat them anew;

transubstantiate.

Sickened flesh flies away
from us, to less malign words.

God sends meat. Each tender
fiber is marbled with fat and salt.

      And so the word returns, saddled with
the errant,
the runaway flesh.   One beginning
seasons another.

Word enters flesh, caustic
or amative. We begin again,
this time with mouths,

interchange of flesh and word.

      The jaw pinned to its mate is endlessly renewed.

1.

The One Big Secret

I admit that grief is arrogant. But

then I am among the most prideful of humans.

A flat assertion is a line

that extends so far as to circle back to itself.

That's how my art has become an evidentiary. My true

feeling is assurance, but assurance at its

bleakest. No one lives inside grief.

My dissections are precise, more meticulous

even than my rage at them. The line, like flesh,

can be made to fold. I relieve those

who are without domicile. This is the manner by

which grief evicts. I have the most scrupulous

knowledge. I act before

my superiority reduces me to tears. No one

has ever reciprocated my mercy. I heard, once, a beggar

say in passing, "faith," and so I painted him into a picture

I placed in a dungeon. I am a flat assertion, line arrowing

to its target and, therefore, not what you are. This grim assurance.

The New Vocation

The body collects aphorisms, as though it were a jar.

That is the world, secured so, and palely organized

according to mysterious function.

I step forward from the system to confess

that I no longer want to whiten

the mystery. I had carried

a knife to cut away armloads of list,

wind blowing. No more this obscurity.

      The body was once fair and loved its excess,

a beauty of retrieval. Yet in so saying, it has

left itself behind, wan

and partial. The speck called

real shrinks in proportion to the truth

said on it. And a willowy body can apportion

its grace to curve even around so small

a thing as this. Benediction or chastisement.

      Function and vocation fight,

physically: I lick myself. I apply tongue

to disappearance. Work and works.

Who was it that mentioned the knife? The sharp

pale paint that the tongue distributes.

Function cuts away the wind, and therefore:

resurrection. And did you know the body

was dead? The real, surrounded by its works,

refers back to the clear container. This term, body,

bleached with overuse, but endlessly flexible

claims its vocation is affect. Stored here,

      riddle is cheek by jowl with question.

I recruit myself as transparent. The real

and its systems forever abating. The mystery

arouses the blade to its calling.

Telescope

Look,

so that the dire

requirement moves beyond

compulsion. The landscape

must be marked as

such light—

and such

the nebulae

I discovered,

a grove on a plot,

a rash on the waist,

an elegant subjugation

of the eye-hole.

My fine, firm

girdle on firmament

sees not just the harshness

of order, but the random

beauty of my markings atop

order, the blotchy hands

encircling the mottled, incurving

lunar torse: peep and purview.

Not what I—what one—

had intended,

the huge bulk of vision

as it violates the universe,

and so small

the cavity of sight.

Wrinkle

There was yet another place to hide in
the compromise.

Something concrete, the real hidey-hole,

a fugitive in its haven,

the stash. My treasure was in the crease.

How my treasure deepened,

like beauty,

absorbed to the skin.

Orrery

One planet is tied to another by human sinew,

the strings of expediency that astral figures pluck.

      Every body knows this exterior.

Knows that pain is a form of vast distance.

The night sky at its deepest hour

is the color of flesh

had we

only the sense to discern. Instead

something more dull than pain

obtrudes, goads—

      a pink inflammatory compressing

bones or

galaxies

in its arthritic fugue. The author

of the body comes apart to

confess fatigue.

What wears away the sky,

like a body come down on itself.

We are inept. There is no cure

but the desire that collapses

ache to a kind of science.

Macchiavelian astronomy.

Some sheerest galaxy drapes over the ghost

exhausted of himself, so tired of

the throe of the body,

who signals the distress of space:

      unfounded, tendon, vein

hurtling, knots.

Less, No Less

Bore holes, nostrils:

self-same. Revolving on

spiral paradise; ultimate beauty

takes in parasite heaven—whiff

this of the deformed face, the cavity

we arise out of.

Rumor

Sometimes the viscera are so quiet
as to clutch their secrets.

This
quiet pleasure
in the sanctuary that lies in wait
in the temple of the body.

That is the rumor.

Therefore to carve a door in such a place

as to make feasible all ingress and egress.

When it is empty, we see finally

the perfect architecture of the cave of the ribs,

and the door sewn onto that
holy violation.

The viscera take us;
we are their vocation.

Taken in holy union
with itself,

the religious rumor

or order that makes a body

and loves with violence. We see
that we must use violence

to love the emptied thing.

2.

This Ideal

I make a model of smut

that we know as constancy.   World peeled off its

succulence.

I make you

to eat this model   if

if

if you knew and loved

as you should.

       The world

shall chastise

–sleight of hand–

by opening your mouth.

Your mouth

I taste—

the model

the world so gladly

ingests.
The sting

of contingency.

       Do you adore—   Do you

do as instructed?

To bear the burden

of the sweet pulp   separated

from its only world—

Only the teacher

       flayed by removal from

the student—
       Obedience

is the true disequilibrium.

       Its ardent example.

Alternate Account

I should explain

in the gothic decorum

of truth that I am

no different than I have

been, but remain troubled

in the dissonance of the pronoun.

Who is it that would present itself

to you as a voice: that gloved or

hooded assertion, dishonestly

anonymous.

Who is authorship otherwise

than a craving for union,

the exquisite politeness

of the isolated voice.

I feign that I walk at

night, but this is, more truthfully,

the swathing of black crepe.

Dressed so. Wry melodrama

of whom? I claim

only my own civility.

But civility's monochromatic

wardrobe could yet perplex

whom I

adopt. The hidden and illicit

progeny of the interview

that did not come to pass

mourns itself off the

borrowings

of my

word or warrant.

Strangers, or the Simultaneous

A man loves a boy, but

it is a boy with a face, fine

and, internal, inside a girl. Awkward

this love, this face and

its sweet neutrality. The man

loves that once he was

a boy. Once

he was a girl and how

he loved the impediment

of body on self,

the human house.

He

loves that once the

surgeon came upon him

to open his doorway and

razed his body to the ground.

The man loves a boy who

was his own dereliction of self.

Such things have structure, the

roof, the foundation, the sweet

neutrality of decrepitude. He

took dirty handfuls of his

feminine self and tamped them

onto some other body. Once,

in the end, was a face molded to

a place. Two structures

merge. The face imagines

architecture, as synthesis,

as what it is not. The surgeon

revisits the scene, its

hermaphroditic wavering.

The man who imparted all

this, he has disappeared,

but for his love, the boy, the girl.

Some quiet is catastrophic,

just as their innocence, a faltering

absence, is an avenue of destruction.

The wayfaring man's sincerity,

reversible and irreversible essences

that demolish

his fine interior affection.

Juggle

See

the color

of the balls and their pattern in air.

We are sometimes attracted to the innards

of the balls who

vault through air. Coercion is juggling's

form. What

depletes their loft in air, then, their

facility for returning

to a capturing hand. Be distracted thus,

bright hue, rubber

colorless gut, all in the scheme

hazardous and

submissive. Between

the flying balls, colorless the tension,

a tightrope made of nothing. Down it

flies the fugitive. The mesmerized

runaway.

Injurious the slick string of the pattern,

the sure pattern that pursues the pattern.

See

the color, the inside, its docility.

The Boy Says

On the shelf

that was my self

rings nothing but

implements of

exit.

On the ledge that

was my self, I hasten

my   bone   horizon

frustrated with

or   not with—

On my measure

such to get set,

remnants of hair,

of growth,   symbol

sheared

away.

Some magic word

despises the child

who was.   Who sports.   This way

he ceases to be.

Most eloquent dissection

          parts with force

I was a boy and now

am not a self.   Horrendous,

says self of self

with glee.

Part from particle.

Abridge   or

or   flee.

This genteel cry

of pain   takes away

the victim, does he,   he

does mature.   I do ugly

progress from this life to

the next—

He knew the forms of

surgery from both ends

there for,   therefore

his elegance.

Above and below

as types of innocence,

all to be treated with knife

and suture.   The divine

perspective is torture

or extraction.   Lovely, oh

lovely shelf now forsaken

of its burden.

As each soul is

and only is

a boy,   I am.

As each artist

would force his way

into the boy,

that is, the idea of

the boy   to be climbed

into.   Shucking off

the artist,   joy   us   horrible.

To prove the idea of boy

as and only

as fit.   The hand

in the exemplary glove

is a fraud. We memorialize

him on his shelf: surfeit   as a garment

outstretched or stretched out.

The self shivered

in its ugly dress. Grown

out or outgrown. He

might escape.   I might

be a child no longer though

he gets a way.   He might claim

this ledge as a blade,

I see   that hastens or deletes his fall.

Figurative fall.   I was my own

perverse boy and the world

stank.   I was the artist that

drew the gown   all complete   on selfhood.

I saw it cheat.

The victim is forbidden despair,   in

that air he makes himself: An "I"

who am puppeting him so that

on this day the cloak I call suspension

will be cut.   Last string   hard   shard

on impact,   for

no despair can fashion

itself to this.   In turn   he

will fall to   this self,

the failure of weight on an empty

shelf.   The garment of the soul   hissing

would rape my insides until

what will grow   up   outgrown—

Extempore

How entirely apt
to the punchline–

who, on a lark,
erases the set-up,

the frame:
husked down

to its pit.
The impulse

of this place
to exsanguinate

the trick–its own
dehydrated self–

could not contribute more
to hilarity. See,

how the impulse
execrates itself

in order
to give pleasure.

3.

Pilfer

I take and then

I extrapolate on the taking

so each take

is at a remove from the last

and the payment we

draw from these confiscations

has no image.

She was not a woman.

There is no red, no white.

Mulct

only. Each diminishment

beatifies the taker

whose interior, like an organ,

swells,

not red, but perhaps

fairer, the generosity

I would claim

for myself. I strew

the edge farther than

the swindle. I myself

had no face, but took

to smiling.

Bitter

Magpie flies over the deepest urban stench
with her bit of glitter.

      Howling sequin,

parallax.

          Now I know you put your body in her nest–
          Is it lucky? Parse

of bauble and spirit.

Magpie's imposter poison—

      Squawking, this small showy object aloft

          on the span above the sewage—

Don't now
fly away–

          The gilt

              you hawk,
      yelp
        and
            showy toy, glint of your lair,

          precarious stink you conceal under your tongue,

    bird, trinket, your flimsy hips

          accommodate the shadow
                    by attracting its sparkle.

Culprit, Victim, Crime, Capture

I trace impure lip, arm,

mole, tit, toe– a trove. Amputate

cap, crap, capture.

Veil time; mutter rapture.

Capitulate. Melt. Placate.

I place part at part.

Reap, rapt, ripe, pure, pare:

I palpate vital matter, repel a leper.

A trial. I meet 'pure' at 'vile.'

A private rite, I lure: cut, care, clap, impale.

Accrue virtue.

Levitate evil.

Melt

This, thus

she lies   a divided pronoun.

The world

wavers   not a hole

smocked, puckered.

Gives a sense   of depth–

melting, it melts,

knife slicing   through softened self.

World in

liquidity   wrangles–

crouches

over.   She

crouches over

herself,   a difficult

situation:

space   situated   in otherwise

solid

mass.

Unexpected definition,

exquisite, extensible

this reprieve   or breach.

Buttery, relented divorce

of hunch over or hover.

Annals

Held in this

fist. History

stored. Thought's perambulation:
the sentry circles

the story.

And if the gaze instills

redemption, whose? Reveille.
Revive the view

clutched in these fingers. Congeries

of fingers. No stopping now—
the fist is in the fingers, the story

revoked by its own clamp.
Knuckling, the

version attacks its own virtue.
Smack

of hand
on slumping fiction.

Said the Supposed Author of All Things

As I dispatched them

to the afterlife, I explained

that the spirit world

is split between male

and female, this decisive

bit of news

      I am enacting the burial

of the crucial body

but no one knows

which is which

I said   Go now,

as though you can't

tell I am not the Almighty

after all, but fluent

in heaven gibberish–

the breasts, testicles

inexplicably gone

      Or go on, disinter:

the heavenly gates

will mutilate

if I am their agent.

4.

Resurrection

If you were to feel faint,

would your flesh step away from you

in revulsion?

As concerns the life that

rises from life,

there is only query, but it must

live inside decay. You might

feel it,

the faintness that comes upon

one when

confronted with the corpse,

or only a reverence for the stink.

Before I died, I was

heartily angry at my own

revolution

     (–a code term

the vulnerable use when

they are revolting). I admit

that there seems little

to query here. Pungeance

will limit

all further trespass.

Trust me not.

If the stench is what

breeds your curiosity,

do not breathe in, or me.

Revisit

Prefatory statements:

–murder is not entirely synonymous with an act of violence

–I believe I was the victim

Memory will serve as meeting ground, but this is troubling because it presupposes that one can perceive a firm sense of ground.

Troubling, because I no longer feel rage,

feel rage enacted on me,

call and response.

Made to wear this cloak of afterness,

what choice have I got but to wonder

if there was truly

a prelapsarian time?

Why does the true black

appear now

so faded and rusty

when the garment would seem to be

the same?

One can run one's finger or blade along the surface, where

surface of skin is the symbol for tension; test time

this way.

Towards those whom I hate the most, I suppress my rage. Its graces
will not be for them.

But for you, who join me in tenderness, I give this gift.
Ergo,

I return.

The picture returns to the picture, the eye returns to its portrayal, the hand writes the words. It pens the words on top of the words, and the voice feels this indentation on the surface, the pure gloss of ink in the rut. The tidy comes back to the horrid mess, calmly,

as a nurse in her pinafore, shirking the fact of the ravage and making its bedding new, undressing and dressing it afresh.

A confession should be inspected toward its purpose. No one
really wants relief.

Always, always the speaker wants to know whom it is, who is being
addressed.

In my head the rhymes clang: relief, belief, thief. I would have wanted to
know
who, whom. Subject of addressed, subjected to.

I confess that this moves too slowly. I envision the creature, the confession,
snatched from behind, and the shocked face that turns back to

look at the grasping hand.

The consequence
of the hand and the folds of garment or
flesh it grasps I confess.

I understand that I appear slow-witted, especially as compares to the swiftness of a former self.

This is the necessary awkwardness, the consequence.

I recall how vividly I felt contempt. This is when

I was victim. This is also

when I did not feel fear.

As it was being enacted, what I felt was regret.

I sniffed the foliage of a former place; I wrapped

my hand around my uncomprehension as though

it were my own wrist. I could scent what had been before

so acutely, and wanted it.

Even now, I wish for a supplement, the purity of form that explanation would take on.

Too ready to adopt the indistinct contours

of its object. Explanation, like its sibling, confession, is too

compliant. That is the site of violence. All that leaks through the
snatching
fingers.

I measure the fault intimately, but it does not

belong to me.

No one can go back to the original site, the scene. That much should be obvious. No one repeats a transgression.

But one by one the parties, who in their aggregate clot into one, did

attempt to return. Presently, nothing is there. Yes, before the Fall, Eden was made up of this incommensurateness. Flicker. Before the

Fall, place itself was an abstraction. Abstract garden of the body. There we were all victims together. The light shone on this alone, piecemeal. Unafraid,

the hand clapped over what one might call the idea of the mouth. Impossible to revisit that muffled exclamation.

Explanation

Some idealized violence
does let off fumes which

the speaker of this moment
breathed in. So accounts this

for the twist of the body
into its new sac of

transporting tissue. Only
in this eros of violence

can paradox breathe
easily; you find the speaker

puts two genders into one
intoxicant called the torso

by which a journey or
a sojourn erupt. The honeyed

balance of indecision is
their intercourse, so the

speaker likes to be itself,
as witness with

a scalpel. Incise fumes. Make
the shoes of the moving soul

reside in its gut. Has the voice
made itself clear: the midsection is

viciously disappointed with
this particular manner of

entanglement, would like to
cut away the distinctness

and close carefully around
something else, blurred, hurried,
hastened savor.

Shroud

Hip
in socket
could find
no better
home,
or
lucent hymn. Yet
remove, as we must,
the   hammer from   the
head   of the nail,   we
then   leave naked   and
interred its
remains
by which one means
that the body exerts more
pressure on its bed than the
shroud does. Filmy as
the terms of the
equation   are, one
imagines   that force:
its meter,   forcing the
head into   what
yields,   takes
cover:
tune's
perturbed
veil.

5.

Derision for the Sleeping

What comes from your body is not sleep
but a word that mocks the synonym.

What you want is the orb I am who
waits upon you because it loves

to wait. Warp of patience, shine
of sleep sanding down sleep,

how we hate each other. Richly,
to exhaustion, I make

the circle of eternity as
the meanest joke a synonym

for shape can know. Know your
body mocked across the equator,

a fraud's girth– night reversed
reserves daylight for the sleepless,

for all that comes from your body,
orb robbed of itself, eternity for

those destitute of pleasure, reward
of heaven rubbed down to the nerve.

Whom Do You Betray by Living?

I return and repine you,

a songbird with molting feathers.

       Or I submerge all qualms.

To you, submerged,

this song engenders

what? The text of the song warping,

and again, a ladder whose

rungs tighten around your lyric

throat. Your qualm-ridden

self-excusing throat. Inside it,

I was to fulfill myself as a task,

and there I was

returning, sufficient and apparently

faithful, where the bird escapes

and the nest is disemboweled.

Can you see me, climbing,

reliable, caught in a tune

hummed in the fleshy

vial of air? Nest

is noose, melodic

haplessness of intention

that falls through–

through. Its job

is to be done, sung

on the limb of

ladder, tree, or

body. The body

chased, inside out

from its own cylinder

of tune. Some alliance

hurts intention as it returns

to where it thought to have

lived. Severe humor

of the recollected task. We do not

bother to kill now. Climbing

is its own sufficiency, alive

and cruel. Self-locating

again

where our natural images,

held under or sloughing,

hold us in contempt.

Answer

Would, then, sleep be
answer or result?

To ensoul the exhausted,

to enter one slothful body
after another

where I see your
legs through your shift

but little of the else of you.

How firmly the answer
closes its eyes so as

to elude what I'd insert. Sleep
seeps out, saline and vague,

whereas the result turns round
with certain fingers to pry open

the eye and the leg. One after

another, doped and transparent,

are those who want so little, who
shorten the shrift of you. To whom

does one show one's fingers, to what
larger fluid spirit does the act of

opening complete? Horde them all up,
then, the corpus, the plural else. See that

you do goggle and whose digits I pull out of
the gist of you, muslin haste, sheer

trade where the result is a mouth, of course,
gagging delicately. The mouth that surely

forces you to dilate, sleeper, my soft
burr, my possession.

The Precise Way In

The fumbler in the dream

turns in sleep. This is the gesture

of exactitude. Fallen

in love, admit or admission, with the

opening, the flesh, the unwisdom

of sleep. Waking, worse,

to new—or some other— flesh. What

one saw there, not a boy, but a girl,

hidden in the folds of itself. Labia

are sleep: jaw is sleep. What comes

out of the coming out, air

in nostrils. Clumsy, this: contradiction

of dream. The conscious turn

in sleep, exacting admission. Body

symmetry, murder, precise wakefulness.

The ones who sleep, they sleep together by creases,

the cut-out paper doll tissue of them. Here is a

chain translucent with awkwardness, the air

forces its way into them. So much cessation,

the dreamer stumbles on it, its novel intimacy.

Acknowledgments

Poems from this collection have appeared in *Aufgabe, Cannibal, Conjunctions, English Language Notes, Fascicles, The New Review, Shiny, Zoland Poetry.*

My thanks also to Wintered Press and Belladonna Books for publishing chapbooks in which earlier versions of some of these poems were published.

Free Verse Editions

Edited by Jon Thompson

13 ways of happily by Emily Carr
& in Open, Marvel by Felicia Zamora
At Your Feet (A Teus Pés) by Ana Cristina César
Between the Twilight and the Sky by Jennie Neighbors
Blood Orbits by Ger Killeen
The Bodies by Christopher Sindt
The Book of Isaac by Aidan Semmens
Canticle of the Night Path by Jennifer Atkinson
Child in the Road by Cindy Savett
Condominium of the Flesh by Valerio Magrelli, trans. by Clarissa Botsford
Contrapuntal by Christopher Kondrich
Country Album by James Capozzi
The Curiosities by Brittany Perham
Current by Lisa Fishman
Day In, Day Out by Simon Smith
Dear Reader by Bruce Bond
Dismantling the Angel by Eric Pankey
Divination Machine by F. Daniel Rzicznek
Erros by Morgan Lucas Schuldt
Fifteen Seconds without Sorrow by Shim Bo-Seon, translated by Chung Eun-Gwi and Brother Anthony of Taizé
The Forever Notes by Ethel Rackin
The Flying House by Dawn-Michelle Baude
Go On by Ethel Rackin
Instances: Selected Poems by Jeongrye Choi, translated by Brenda Hillman, Wayne de Fremery, & Jeongrye Choi
The Magnetic Brackets by Jesús Losada, translated by Michael Smith & Luis Ingelmo
Man Praying by Donald Platt
A Map of Faring by Peter Riley
The Miraculous Courageous by Josh Booton
No Shape Bends the River So Long by Monica Berlin & Beth Marzoni
Overyellow, by Nicolas Pesquès, translated by Cole Swensen
Physis by Nicolas Pesquès, translated by Cole Swensen
Pilgrimage Suites by Derek Gromadzki
Pilgrimly by Siobhán Scarry

About the Author

Elizabeth Robinson is the author of multiple collections of poetry, including the National Poetry Series winner, *Pure Descent,* and the Fence Modern Poets Prize winner, *Apprehend.* Her mixed-genre meditation, *On Ghosts,* was a finalist for the Los Angeles Times book award in poetry. Robinson was twice the Hugo Fellow at the University of Montana, and has received residency fellowships from the Maison Dora Maar, the Djerassi Resident Artists Program, the Marin Headlands Center for the Arts, and the MacDowell Colony. Robinson has also received grants from the Fund for Poetry and the Foundation for Contemporary Arts. Her poetry has appeared in such anthologies as *American Hybrid, The Norton Anthology of Postmodern American Poetry,* and *The Best American Poetry of 2002.* She works as the homeless navigator for Boulder Municipal Court and teaches at Lighthouse Writers' Workshop.

Photograph of the author by John Sarsgard.
Used by permission.

CPSIA information can be obtained
at www.ICGtesting.com
Printed in the USA
FFOW03n1033070218
44907681-45116FF